READING'S FORGOTTEN CHILDREN

The story of the Reading Board Schools, 1871 – 1902

R. S. Bray, BA (Hons), Open University.

Published by the author at
10 Lyme Grove
Tilehurst
READING
Berkshire
RG31 5AJ

ISBN 0954203569

Design and Preparation by
KRB Publications
2 Denewulf Close
BISHOPS WALTHAM
Hants
S032 1GZ

Printed by the Amadeus Press

©R.S. Bray 2003.

Battle School 1928/9

The Junior School entrance to Alfred Sutton School. This was originally the Wokingham Road Board School.

Foreword by Nigel Bray

The names Alfred Sutton, E.P. Collier and George Palmer will be immediately associated by Reading people with well-established schools in the town. Yet how many local people know that these successful businessmen, some of whose industries such as Sutton's Seeds and Huntley & Palmer's biscuits became world famous, were local pioneers in the movement to provide and manage education for children from the poorest families ?

The Board Schools introduced by W.E. Forster's Education Act of 1870 represented the first serious attempt by central and local Government to see that all children of between five and 14 were educated. It must have been a culture shock for the first generation of children from ordinary backgrounds who had to go to school on a regular basis and whose parents could no longer use their offspring as free labour.

It is 100 years since the Board School system was superseded but many of the problems it faced – suitability of buildings, content of lessons, academic results, discipline, truancy – are live issues today. My father's research has uncovered how teachers, pupils, parents and administrators struggled with these problems in Reading. He has drawn on a wealth of sources and his long experience as a local teacher.

Contents

Author's note and Introduction	5
Ch. 1 The Board School Elections	7
Ch. 2 Recruiting the Children	11
Ch. 3 The First Board Schools	15
Ch. 4 The Pioneers	25
Appendix 1 – Reading Board Schools in 1902, as listed in Kelly's Directory for Reading, 1903.	31
Appendix 2 – Average Attendance at Reading Board Schools in the year up to 31 October, 1902, as shown in Kelly's Directory for Reading, 1903.	31

(Cover photo: Children at Battle School, 1928. (Mrs. B. Petherbridge collection).

(Opposite page: Alfred Sutton Primary School entrance, July 2002. This school was originally Wokingham Road Board School (Nigel Bray).

A contemporary illustration from 'Punch' – Vol. 75, 1878. The cartoon referred to the subject of Education with the Inspector of Schools stating, " It strikes me that Teacher of yours retains little or no hold upon the attention of children&". The debate of the period also centring around teachers being paid by results. 'Performance related pay' is then not a recent initiative.

Author's Note

What I have attempted here are some glimpses of Victorian attitudes to elementary education in Reading, Berkshire. It is not a definitive history of local Board Schools in general, or of any one school in particular.

The views of people in authority, of Principal Teachers, School Inspectors and parents have been my special concern.

I also owe a very great debt for the kindly assistance I have received from the staffs of Tilehurst Library, the Reading Central Library, the Berkshire Record Office and from local teachers too numerous to mention individually, for which I hope to be forgiven.

Finally I wish to acknowledge the inspiration of the Open University in accepting my thesis on Attitudes to Board School Education, which was the starting point for my endeavours.

Introduction

The history of English education is like a patchwork quilt of many diverse and uneven strands, ranging from monastic foundations to the early Nineteenth Century ventures, Dame Schools, Private Adventure Schools, High Anglican and Nonconformist academies.

Significantly, for the development of elementary education in Reading, a Ragged School Union was launched in 1845 and a Boys' Ragged School was started in St. Giles Parish in 1847. Up to 40 men and young boys were attending the Ragged School in 1870 at the time of the introduction of Mr. Forster's Education Act. It was from these humble beginnings that Mr. Sutton who had worked selflessly in the Ragged School movement, was asked by the newly elected members of the Reading School Board, if he would carry on his mission work, by connecting it with the Board's education plans for the Newtown area.

The view was widely held however, both locally and nationally, that the teaching of children was a private parental responsibility. Parents were expected to provide food, clothing and shelter for their offspring, and society generally expected that private rather than "state" intervention was required. This was well illustrated in 1871 by Mrs. (later Dame) Millicent Fawcett, who wrote that from the point of view of state education it would probably be the wisest course of action to let the children of those parents who could not afford school fees to remain uneducated. She continued, that in her opinion, the process of natural selection would gradually force uneducated people out of existence !

Fortunately for the future, William Edward Forster MP saw matters differently, for in the conclusion of his speech bringing his Education Bill to Parliament he stated that 'upon the speedy provision of elementary education depends industrial prosperity ... upon the speedy provision of education depends also our national power.' *

- Hansard series (iii) volume 199 1870.

Parliament voted in Forster's Bill in a compromise form resulting from terrific battles between High Churchmen and Dissenters. A year later, on 25 February, 1871 the Mayor of Reading announced that an order had been received from the Education Department for a school board to be set up in the town within 28 days of the receipt of the order. The struggle to educate the poorest sections of the poor was about to begin.

Important Dates in Education

1810	Lancastrian Free School founded on east side of Southampton Street.
1812	National (Anglican) Schools established for the parishes of St. Mary's and St. Laurence's.
1833	Government grant of £20,000 for building of National and Dissenter Schools.
1835	Infant school in Hosier Street, Reading.
1836	St. Giles National School founded.
1846	School Inspectors appointed nationally.
1847	A 'Ragged School' started in St. Giles parish.
1863	Revised Code (payment by results).
1865–1923	Greyfriars School.
1869	National Liberal Education League formed.
1870	Forster's Education Act.
1871	Reading Board Schools in Silver Street and Coley Street.
1872	Katesgrove Lane School opened.
1874	Reading School Board appoints a Medical Officer.
1876	Limited elementary education compulsory.
1878	First meeting of the Tylehurst School Board.
1880	Grovelands Board School opened, then in Tilehurst Parish.
1883	Oxford Road Board School opened.
1890	Tilehurst Board School (later Park Lane School).
1891	Building of Battle School is approved. Education freed from school fees.
1895	Over one million children in Board Schools nationally.
1899	Swansea Road Board School (later E.P. Collier School) opened
1902	The Balfour Education Act abolishes Board Schools, which become a Local Authority responsibility.

Chapter 1

THE BOARD SCHOOL ELECTIONS

Many local people at the time hoped for an uncontested election, as reported from Blackburn in the Reading Mercury of 14 January, 1871. Here, although 26 candidates had originally been nominated, these were somehow reduced to 13, the actual number of places on the Blackburn Schools' Committee Board.

In Reading an inaugural meeting was held in the Council Chamber, convened by circular for the purpose of taking steps if possible, to prevent a contested election for membership of the proposed School Board. J.H. Wilson of Whitley Hill was Chairman; also present were Alderman Palmer, Mr. Simmonds and Mr. G.W. Colebrook.

The Chairman hoped that a list of names could be fixed upon for the School Board, which would be acceptable to the town, as representing the thoughts and feelings of the inhabitants. It was anticipated that a list of suitable gentlemen would avoid the sad results of a contested election (cries of Hear ! Hear !).

It was noted that the vicars of the three parishes had been invited to the meeting, but they preferred not to be there, as was the case also with other clergymen, and some nonconformists.

It was agreed that the scheme of representation should embrace all parties, whether social, political or religious. The object was to avoid scrambling for seats, unnecessary expense and a possible result which might be serious for the cause of Education, to the rates and social order ... the feeling "out of doors" was that the School Board should be composed of lay members (Hear ! Hear !), that neither clergymen or nonconformist ministers should have a seat on it.

Mr. Wilson admitted that the clergy were pioneers in education and were experienced in school matters, but he denied that they had any vested rights in matters of education, which other people did not possess. He thought that the pressure of clergymen on the Board would be a continual element of discord.

It was significant that on the day prior to the meeting (3 March, 1871) the Nonconformists had met and decided they would not put up candidates for the School Board, provided no Anglican clergymen came forward. (Hear ! Hear !) *

Further Meetings and Opinions

Amongst other gatherings, was one advertised by handbills to be held at the Primitive Methodist Schoolroom in London Street, as reported in the Reading Mercury of 11 March, 1871. Here the friends of unsectarian education and working men were urged to attend. When the names of J.H. Wilson, Alfred Sutton, Mr. Simmonds and others were read out as members of the Church party, it was agreed that it was up to noncomformists and working men to put forward their nominees for places on the board.

* extracts from the Microfilm records of the Reading Mercury, 4 March, 1871.

The general feeling expressed at this meeting was that the right men for the job should be elected, whether churchmen or dissenters no matter, so long as they were the right people, but if unsectarian education meant education without the Bible, the meeting was against it (Hear ! Hear !).

Mr. Sutton was strongly recommended to the meeting because of his work for Ragged Schools, and so great was the interest shown, that this meeting was immediately followed by another in the Council Chamber, but because of the large attendance an adjournment was made to the Town Hall.

The Association of Church Schoolmasters also held a meeting, at which the need to keep down the rates was stressed; this factor was also mentioned in the election advertisements of two of the candidates for the School Board, unfortunately unnamed in this report. These anonymous candidates also maintained that they were for judicious liberality and economy with efficiency, in fact the best of all worlds ! The ratepayers, they remarked, did not want a higher rate for education than for sanitary purposes.

Significant of thinking at the time was the Rev. Armstrong who at the Church Schoolmasters' meeting, stated that the Church Schools would continue to be preferred to the proposed Board Schools, as they were already known to the parents. The rate–aided schools, on the other hand, would attract the same class of children as were to be found in the Ragged Schools.

On 18 March, 1871, according to the excellent coverage given in the Reading Mercury, there was yet another meeting, this time at Mr. Hutt's Repository, where the Rev. J.F. Stevenson (later elected to the Reading School Board) said "he somewhat deprecated the compulsory powers of the 1870 Education Act, for the father was responsible not only to God but to society for the way he brought up his children. If a man would not be influenced by moral suasion, and the fear of public opinion, to give his children the benefits of education so easily within his grasp", the law, he maintained, should compel him. Still he was more for compulsory education by moral force.

Mr. Colebrook (subsequently not elected to the Board) spoke at the West Street Hall meeting, to the effect that any government which was called into power must be progressive. He was glad that the government was wise enough and strong enough to be equal to the occasion, when they saw that a school board was necessary. He was afraid that they would find in Reading a considerable number of children whose parents were so poor as not to be able to pay for their children's education. This could be met by the ratepayers remitting fees, he said.

The Candidates

Mr. George John Wait of Rose Cottage, London Road, offered himself for election to the School Board as follows,

'It having been decided that we shall have an Educational School Board, I beg respectfully to offer myself as a candidate. Having from an early period in life felt a deep interest in the moral welfare of the people, both in the material and educational point of view, I know that the essence of tuition lies in the inward reception of the sublime truths of the Bible, and I am decidedly opposed to what is termed the secular view of the question, believing that merely to sharpen the intellect is simply to make men clever without making them useful members of society.'

After more remarks about the teaching of the Bible in school, Mr. Wait concluded, 'Having had business experience extending over a period of thirty years, I should only, if elected, support measures tending to keep the rates for the support of the schools at the least point combined with efficiency.'

In spite of these sentiments Mr. Wait came out bottom of the poll with a mere twenty–four votes, some two thousand behind the successful candidates.

In a local press editorial prior to the election, Mr. Sutton was highly supported, as was the Rev. Cust, whereas a local ironmonger, R.D. Catchpool (champion of minorities) and Mr. Colebrook (butcher) were not endorsed. Mr. Colebrook was referred to as a champion of Future Board Schools, who envisaged them taking over from the Church Schools, a view which the press did not share because of the possible effect this might have on the local rates.

The Berkshire Chronicle forecast that a majority of church-men voting for the Church Party, would secure the return of the Rev. Cust, Rev. Stevenson and Messrs. Monck, Sutton and Wilson.

The Board School elections made possible in some areas of the country a greater degree of local democratic participation, although at first no–one in Reading classified as a working–class man appeared with the exception of Mr. Jesse Herbert, a Primitive Methodist and treasurer of the local Working Men's Liberal Association. Unlike some northern areas, no women candidates came forward until the arrival of Miss D.J. Ridley and Miss E.M. Sutton in 1901.

At first there were two parties or factions represented in Reading, people with Church as their background, and the Noncomformists. By 1892 the Committee had representatives from a new force – members of the Social Democratic Federation which had a very strong following in the town. People with this allegiance were instructed how to vote and, because of their numbers and discipline, secured representation for the SDF. One of this party, Mr. J.F. Hodgson, while serving on the Reading School Board, was an early advocate of equal pay for teachers, a claim which was not taken seriously until well on in the twentieth century.

Election Results

On 21 March, 1871 the Mayor of Reading declared the Board School election results as follows (occupations and addresses of candidates are as listed by the Berkshire Chronicle):

Elected

Alfred Sutton (Seedman. Greenlands, Redlands Road, Reading)	3,642
William Payne (Vicar of St. John's, Reading)	3,521
George Palmer (Biscuit manufacturer. The Acacias, London Road, Reading)	3,361
Joseph Henry Wilson (Gentleman. Whitley Hill, Whitley, Reading)	3,196

Rev. Arthur Purey Cust (Vicar of St. Mary's, Reading)	2,750
Rev. John. Stevenson (Dissenting Minister. Clarendon Terrace, South Street, Reading)	2,607
Jesse Herbert (Boot Maker. Horn Street, St. Giles Parish, Reading)	2,334
Ebenezer West (Headmaster. Amersham Hall School, Caversham)	2,330
John B. Monck (Esquire and Magistrate. Coley Park, Reading)	2,231

Not elected

George Colebrook (Butcher. London Street, Reading)	2,053
Thomas Masterman (Gentleman)	162
Richard Catchpool (Ironmonger. Living in Eldon Square, Reading)	75
George Wait (Commission Agent. Rose Cottage, London Road, Reading)	24

His Worship the Mayor expressed his personal satisfaction, after the election of the first Reading School Board:

'I feel I must congratulate the town upon having obtained a most satisfactory Board. I do not know whether there may be much necessity for their labours here. I do not anticipate that their labours will be laborious or onerous. The town is better provided with schools than most places.' *

Let the facts speak for themselves. Within three months of this statement, the newly constituted Reading School Board discovered that out of a total of 62 elementary schools of all kinds in existence, 33 were efficient and 29 could be classified as not efficient. The report added benevolently,

'We wish to speak of them with all consideration as beneficial, but estimated by the requirements of the Education Act of 1870 we feel reluctantly bound to state our conviction that they are defective, some in teaching power, others in school apparatus, others from the nature of their premises and surroundings......all falling short of the requirements of the present standard of elementary education.' $

* Berkshire Chronicle, 25 March, 1871.
$ Volume I, Reading School Board Committee Minute Book, June 1871.

Silver Street west side, looking southwards, 1887.

(Reading Borough Library)

Chapter 2

RECRUITING THE CHILDREN

On 19 April, 1871 by order of the newly elected School Board, their clerk Mr. Samuel Preston issued a circular to parents pointing out that 'under the provisions of the Education Act of 1870 parents of every child between the ages of 5 and 13 years residing in the Borough should cause such child to attend school.'

It added that the great advantage of sending children between 3 and 5 years to Infant Schools would prevent the necessity for the appointment of School Attendance Officers, and the consequent expense to the ratepayers for compelling school attendance.

In conclusion the circular stated, 'in making this appeal to parents the Board are activated by a sincere desire for the good of the children, and they would rather see by the voluntary efforts of the parents that they appreciated the great advantages for education, than that by their apathy and indifference it should become necessary to enforce the compulsory powers which the Board possess for the attainment of the same object !'

Baby Admissions

Unfortunately, the practice of admitting children to Board Schools in Reading under the age of 3 years was often resorted to, on account of the views held on the Board School Management Committee 'if they were not admitted the number of scholars will be unadvisedly reduced.' An example of this from the Silver Street School as late as 1896, shows that Letitia Hardie, described as a Baby Monitress, had so distinguished herself as to be recommended by the school teacher who supervised her work, for a position as a Pupil Teacher. So diligent and attentive to her duties was she apparently, that 'she should be allowed to be presented at the next inspection of the school, for examination as a candidate for engagement as a pupil teacher.' It was agreed to make a representation to the School Management Committee to this effect.

This information came, in the first instance, from a sub–committee appointed by the School Management Committee who provided two members each month to visit Board Schools. Minutes of these visits covered the state of the school, reports on maintenance, discipline, and all matters which generally affected the smooth running of the individual school being visited.

School Attendance Officers

Reading's response to its School Board's circular was in many cases far from satisfactory. Truancy was commonplace, even mass exodus for summer work or a visiting circus. Epidemics, general ill–health and the constant battling of parents endeavoring to get their children into employment, led to advertisements in 1873 via the local press for 'a respectable and intelligent School Attendance Officer'. There were originally 61 applicants ! When this was whittled down to a short list of four, two were selected. Just over a year later, one of them was requesting an increase in his salary because of the extra time at night spent in writing up reports, plus the extra expense of wear on shoes and clothing. The Board approved an increase from £75 per annum to £85 while an Assistant Attendance Officer's money was increased from 15 to 17 shillings a week..
Extracts from School Attendance Officer reports are revealing– for example on 6 November, 1872 it was reported, 'I have sent 15 more parents to the Destitute Children's Clothing Aid Society' and more significantly,

'I have sent from the streets during school hours 26 boys and 24 girls to their respective schools. I have spoken to and admonished 58 other boys and 21 girls in the streets, who within the specified ages were non–attendants at the schools. I visited a clergyman's house and the Superintendent of Police with reference to three unmanageable boys.......I have divided the town into 12 districts.....I regret that my efficiency is not furthered by prompt and ready means of sending to school the number of destitute children who daily come under my observation.'

This report was passed to the Reading School Board in a letter covering the period from November to December 1872.

One possible solution was an application to the School Board to get the Board of Guardians to take over responsibility for children who, because of extreme poverty, did not attend school. The Guardians replied that as a rule they could not undertake to pay school fees.

In Coventry some schools were charging 6d a week fees, reduced in practice to one penny a week for the children of labourers, two pence a week for a shoemaker's children and three pence weekly for a farmer's child. In Reading, the school fees were two pence for the first child in a family and one penny for each additional child. Teachers were originally authorised by the Reading School Board to refuse admission to children who appeared on Monday mornings without their school pence. Children so excluded often failed to return, or reappeared days later, still without their money. Even as late as May 1890 it was reported to the Board that 255 attendances had been lost at Grovelands School, owing to children being sent home for non–payment of fees.

In 1872 the Destitute Children's Aid Committee paid the school fees of some children, supplemented by private charity, and a payment of loans for shoes and clothing to enable impoverished children to go to school. The Board of Guardians was again approached as to the possibility of paying the school pence of the poorest children in the town. At first there was a blank refusal, but a year later in 1873 the Guardians were required by law to assist needy scholars.

The Board's income was not, of course, mainly from fees but from the town rates, amounting in 1876 to some £1,450. By 1879 the figure had reached £3,000 which meant an education rate of fivepence halfpenny in the pound. The amount of these ever rising rate precepts was naturally resented by many ratepayers, and much was made in the local Liberal and Conservative papers of the anger of ratepayers, over the alleged extravagance of the Reading School Board. On the one hand there was a feeling for better education, and on the other, the conviction that the rates were far too high. Decades later, at the end of the Board School system, the Berkshire Chronicle of 20 September, 1902 hoped that the new education authorities (under the proposed Balfour Act) would 'not be quite so ready to be generous with other people's money.' They welcomed, however, the new Government proposals which they described as 'welcome to long–suffering ratepayers in both town and country.'

Mr. E. West, a Board Committee member, wrote to the Reading Observer, pointing out that the Board School Committee had a statutory obligation to supply any needs in accommodation and schooling but that they worked under very rigid limitation from the Education Department of 'Their Lordships' in London.

From the mid 1890s, the Social Democratic Federation members of the Board, by now a lively and vociferous force for progress as they saw it, took the stand that they put the welfare of the children first, and saving the ratepayers' money second.

The Reading Observer commented that the alarming increase in rates were due to the fact that the town was experiencing a steadily increasing number of children to be taught, in fact an extra 200 children each year; they also noted that Reading had some 8,000 children each year on school registers, while other boroughs with a similar rateable value had only to provide for 1,500 children. Help to the rates should be given, the Observer stated, from Government sources.

Non Attendance

Health reasons, objections to the conduct of certain teachers, aesthetical reasons, lack of shoes or proper clothing were some of the excuses made to the visiting School Attendance Officers, in attempts to escape prosecution for truancy. There were, however, other factors, as in the case of Thomas Gough who one Wednesday evening in 1872 was observed 'intoxicated in the street', as recorded in the Silver Street School Log Book. From the same Log Book, is the record of two other scholars J. Prior and J. Huggins who were absent from school 'being in the Newbury Lock–Up.' The crimes were not described, but on a subsequent occasion in August 1876 Huggins was imprisoned for stealing fruit.

Industrial Training Schools

For incorrigible offenders, there were the well–established Truant Schools, such as the Certified Industrial Truant School at Plymouth, to which boys and girls were sent from Reading under police escort, for an indefinite period.

If the children behaved well, they might be released on licence to their original schools. If they reoffended, by persistent truancy and bad behaviour, they could, in theory, be returned to the Truant School.

One 12–year–old boy was arrested for petty larceny in Reading, released, reoffended and was again recommitted to the Truant School he had previously attended. When they refused to have him back, the Reading School Board decided to refer him to the local magistrates for authority to send him to a Truant School elsewhere.

On 2 November 1894, Kate Ambrose, aged 15, was released on licence from the Certified Industrial School, Leeds, where she had been detained for two years. Altogether 13 truancy cases in Reading were referred to Industrial Schools in the years 1899–1900.

Recruiting the Children

Truants and the Law

Throughout the first three decades in the history of the Reading Board Schools a constant battle raged between those set in authority over them, and feckless parents.

William Gould, for example, was committed on 24 April 1873 by local magistrates to the Barnes' Home Industrial School at Heaton Mersey for four years, under the terms of the Industrial Schools Act, at the cost to the Reading School Board of one shilling per week. The order of the JPs fixed the payment to be made by Gould's father at two shillings per week.

Fanny Clark, aged 11 years, the daughter of George Clark, chimney sweep and beerhouse keeper of Hosier Street, 'was reported to the Committee as guilty of offences which render her amenable to the Industrial Schools Act of 1866.' ......'Finding after investigation of the circumstances, that there are strong reasons why she should be sent to an Industrial School, your Committee has agreed to recommend the Board to resolve to contribute towards her maintenance at an Industrial School upon the Justices committing her to one. On enquiry as to what schools are available for Girls, it has been ascertained that she may be committed to the Dorset Home and Certified Industrial School at Poole, free of expense to the Board at present, and with only the prospective expense of an outfit in the event of her going from the school to domestic service, and therefore under these circumstances your Committee can have no doubts of the propriety of her being committed to the above named Industrial School, and they recommend that the Justices be requested to commit her there accordingly.'

'It was resolved unanimously, on the motion of Mr. Wilson, the Chairman, seconded by Mr. Herbert, that the paragraph in the Report of the Committee with respect to the commitment of Fanny Clark to the Dorset Home and Industrial School be adopted, and the same was adopted accordingly.'

This case arose originally in connection with theft from the Broad Street Chapel, Reading. The magistrates were averse to sentencing the girl to prison in view of her age.

Parents who sought to beat the system sometimes forged birth certificates, gave wrong information about a child's age, jobs pending, delicate health, or in one case quoted incapacity for learning as reasons for non attendance in school.

Fines averaging two shillings and sixpence were the usual remedy, although these did not deter a Reading bargeman who was prosecuted, over the years, no less than 34 times !

A School Attendance Committee was set up to sift through parental applications for school exclusions. Many parents were anxious that their children aged 11, 12 or 13 should be out at work. Permission was often granted if the child concerned had passed the required standard in school, if a suitable kind of employment was definitely available, and if the child returned to school for examination by one of Her Majesty's Inspectors at the next annual inspection.

In one case of parental illness, a month's leave was absence was requested; the Board allowed two weeks. Children who were discovered to be working for shopkeepers, or other employers illegally, were often returned to school, after a warning to the employers.

One boy of school age was sent to work at Huntley and Palmer's Biscuit Factory. As his mother would not send him back to school, nor produce a record of his age, the Board School Attendance Officer reported 'I took his name to the factory, and he was dismissed. He is now at school.' (Report by N G Ford, Attendance Officer to the Reading School Board in 1874).

A further five children who also worked illegally at the Biscuit Factory, were successfully dealt with in the same fashion as before. In no instances, are there are any records of any employer in Reading ever having been prosecuted for breaking the law on school attendance.

James Hunt was summoned to prove that his son was what he stated him to be, namely over 13 years of age and not eligible for schooling. Hunt did not appear to answer the summons, and a warrant was issued for his arrest. He was then produced in court, but brought no proof of the boy's actual age. He was then allowed another week by magistrates to get proof. He further failed to present himself in court at the time appointed, and another warrant was issued for his re-arrest. He was then sentenced to seven days imprisonment.

In another case Joseph Toms was allowed five days in which to pay fines for the non attendance of his children in school. As Toms subsequently failed to appear, a warrant was issued and he was then locked up for a short time, after which the fine was paid. Altogether, he had a record of five prosecutions, fines being eventually paid by him of five shillings on four occasions, and once of two shillings and sixpence.

Pupils were sometimes excluded from school because the school or certain standards were said to be full; then the Attendance Officer was advised to act as considerately as possible in the circumstances. Sadly, Reading Board School children in the last quarter of the 19th Century were excluded from school on occasion because of their verminous and dirty state.

Jacob Harris, for example, was reported by the Attendance Officer as being out of work, with his whole family in a state of destitution, the children partially naked. He was prosecuted for breach of the relevant bye–laws, the case was referred to the Relieving Officer and the Medical Officer of the town 'but nothing was done.' The summons was later withdrawn and the Bench awarded Harris five shillings from the poor box. The children did not come to school but their father obtained employment.

By 1876 half the total child population nationally was under compulsion, while the percentage attendance in Reading sometimes reached 84, but certainly not reliably so for long periods.

There was in the period up to 1902 a consistently improving standard of attendance in Board Schools, compared with the percentage figures for Voluntary Schools. Reading's Board Schools were also ahead of the national position, eg in 1901 the attendance figure for England overall was 82.06 % while that for Reading Board Schools was 84.5 % (see Appendix 2 for 1902 figures by school).

After 1877 a new bye–law stated that no boy or girl under 10 years of age, may go to work until the age of 14 years. A child could not go to work unless he or she had passed an examination by an H.M.I. in the 5th standard of work.

When 'free' education was introduced in 1891, it was thought necessary for the Board to remind employers and parents of the legal position. In 1901 another local bye–law ensured that no children under 12 years of age were to be employed. Children from 12 to 13 years could be employed only if they had passed Standard VII in a written examination. Children aged between 13 and 14 years could be 'beneficially employed' if they had made 350 attendances, in not more than two schools in each year, for five years.

After they had reached the age of 14, pupils were exempt from compulsory school attendance, but any child under 14 years of age was required to hold a certificate of proficiency, before being released into the outside world of employment.

Transfer of Pupils between Schools

Removal of children from Board Schools to 'Dame Schools' or 'Private Adventure Schools' was deprecated by the Reading School Board, although the magistrates took the view that freedom of choice for parents must be allowed.

The Reading School Board on the other hand stated that in their opinion, these other schools were not efficient within the terms of the 1870 Education Act, and that children attending other schools did not necessarily put in regular attendances.

The number of these schools in Reading was noted as being on the increase, and that they were, according to the Board, an evasion of the Council bye–laws. In addition, such practices were thought to be seriously impeding the work of education in Denominational, as well as Board Schools.

The Board Schools' Committee wrote to 'Their Lordships of Her Majesty's most Honourable Privy Council, listing their objections to the creaming–off of pupils to the private schools. They requested that a competent Government official should decide the question of efficiency, or otherwise, of the Private Adventure and 'Dame' Schools in the Borough of Reading. No action from on high appears to have been taken, but over the years improvement in success and status of the Board Schools led to the reduction, and eventually complete disappearance, of 'Dame' and 'Adventure' Schools in the town.

Chapter 3

THE FIRST BOARD SCHOOLS

A small sub–committee was set up to visit the districts of Coley, Somerset Place and Silver Street, which were regarded as being most in need of Board Schools. Previously, the Reading School Board had agreed that the three Town Sergeants should visit those houses whose occupants 'are of the class for whom elementary schools are established'.

At Coley, rooms in which a night school was held, under the control of the Vicar of St. Mary's, were inspected, also the rooms nearby known as Coley School. These rooms were considered suitable for the purposes of Board School education. The Trustees were found to be willing to grant the use of the rooms at a rent of £20 per annum. The sub–committee recommended that a Board School be opened in the Coley School Rooms, on a seven–year lease.

In Silver Street, Mr. Sutton's Mission School premises were inspected, with a view to their being used as Board School accommodation. It was decided to purchase the freehold of the Silver Street Day School, and to erect such other buildings as might be necessary.

For Coley School, on its transfer to the authority of the Board Schools' Committee, a Certificated Master was to be appointed at a salary of £90 per annum, with a Mistress for the Girls' School at £60 per annum. A Mistress for the Infants' School was required at £55, plus two shillings and sixpence for each child for whom the Government capitation attendance grant should be obtained. Applications for these teaching appointments were to be advertised in the School Board's Chronicle and the National Society's paper.

Demolition of old cottages in progress at Silver Street, believed to be in 1925. (Reading Borough Library)

Pell Street, Katesgrove, named after Miss Pell, who sold land to the Reading School Board for the building of Katesgrove School.   (Author).

The first temporary Board School was opened in January 1872, the Coley Street School, followed in March by the Silver Street School. In July another temporary Board School was established in Katesgrove, not far from the site of Miss Pell's 'Dame' School.

The Reading School Board, and Her Majesty's Inspectorate, felt the need of Junior and Infant Schools, or Junior Mixed, rather than separate schools, as a matter of necessity, as well as policy: Katesgrove School was to be continued for one year as a Mixed Infant and Junior School for 60 children (April 1872).

The Children

The first Board School children were seen but not allowed to be heard. Their story surfaces occasionally, and dramatically, in the pages of School Log Books, and only then because some Head Teacher had ignored Revised Code Article 50 which stipulated that no reflections or opinions of a general character were to be entered in school records.

The physical state of many of these children are sometimes recorded, e.g. ' sent Charles Garraway home as he came without shoes, and his clothes and person so filthy.' or
'I have been unusually tried this week by the ragged, braceless, buttonless state of some of the boys, their mothers telling me that the men spend their money, on drink, that should be spent on the children........sent one dirty family home, but to no purpose, their mother being out at work.' (Silver Street Infant School Log Book, 1874).

Problems continued into 1882, when on 8 November it was reported to the Board and recorded in their Minutes that a number of pupils from the Silver Street School who had been absent hop–picking, returned to school in a state of uncleanliness which rendered them unfit to associate with the other children.

The Board's solution was that in the case of children attending school in a dirty state, the Managers and Teachers were to have them 'properly washed by the Caretaker, or some other suitable person, and to pay such a person 4d per child on each occasion the duty shall be performed.'

In 1899 the situation still sometimes recurred, when the cleansing of children by a suitable person was again authorised, otherwise the children were to be excluded from school, but now for the first time, the consent of the parents was also mentioned.

Dirt was not the only hazard, as complained of in the Silver Street School Log Book in February 1873: 'I gave my Arithmetic lesson at 11 a.m. instead of at 10 o'clock, Miss Johnson and myself having been troubled by vermin.' Children and teachers closeted in large numbers in makeshift rooms suffered greatly from the cold in winter, e.g. 'the Infant Rooms being imperfectly warmed', this from Grovelands School. At the same school in 1883 a visiting Inspector reported that 'the school appears to suffer considerable inconvenience from the absence of any means of lighting' and, more seriously for the teachers concerned, it was noted that there were two inaccuracies in registers, later the subject of a special warning letter to Grovelands School from this Inspector.

On the same theme of light, the Principal Teacher of Coley Street School wrote a letter to the Reading School Board on 9 April, 1881, from which the following extract is significant: 'During the winter much time is wasted, and the discipline suffers in consequence of the darkness of the rooms.....it will be worse than in the past, as the ground above the school has been built upon, and there is a greater obstruction of light from the west....As the Committee were unable to recommend the Board to provide gas lighting' (although street gas lights had existed in Reading since 1819), 'I would wish the Committee to take into consideration the advisability of putting in two more windows.'

The First Board Schools

Trolleybuses pass the now demolished Grovelands School, 1965.

(David Hall).

The Committee replied to the Principal Teacher that they needed further time for consideration of the matter. In the meantime, they suggested that the walls of the Boys' Schoolroom should be washed and coloured, as on financial grounds they could not take any other immediate action. Conditions in the Board Schools for the children and their teachers in the first two decades were often very poor, with cold and wet weather frequently recorded in School Log Books as being the main reasons for non attendance. When it was very cold, children were allowed to sit round the fire, while in excessively hot weather they often slept, the schoolroom floors being sprinkled with water.

'Too cold and wet for drill' reads one log book entry for April 1888. The Coley Street School Log Book in January 1885 mentions that the Head sent the boys to drill 'although the weather was very unsuitable, as they have missed three drills out of the last seven, owing to the cold and wet.'

Sickness and chronic physical weakness also affected the schools. In 1872 there were two deaths from 'disease of the brain' (meningitis?) amongst the infants, and much rheumatic fever, while as late as December 1898 Battle School was closed by the Reading Sanitary Authority in an attempt to halt the spread of measles. A severe epidemic of whooping cough and many cases of ringworm came to light, and the general state of uncleanliness among the young was tackled in the first instance by the provision of washbasins, combs and towels.

Help for the 'inner man' or rather child, came with the realisation that some Board School children were arriving hungry if not literally starving, as the Board was urged to provide free meals for the children of the unemployed. In severe weather twenty of the more deserving, out of 100 pupils, were provided with a pint of soup and bread for four days at the Rising Sun Coffee Tavern. This practice of occasional free meals was discontinued in 1893.

Further problems arose from exemptions made by the transfer of children from one standard, class or form to a higher standard. These exemptions were considered necessary because 'there are two or three children in the school who cannot be taught by the ordinary methods of instruction on account of weak intellect.' In 1890 Elizabeth Cox, a pupil at Grovelands School in Standard Two had to be witheld from the Standard Three examination as she was very delicate, and mentally deficient. 'Weakness of brain' was given as the reason for a girl at Katesgrove School being treated exceptionally in Standard Two of the school. Usually, scholars reported as deaf and dumb, and or mentally defective were sometimes provided for in a special room, segregated, as was the case at Oxford Road Board School in 1901. Even more exceptionally, there is one recorded case of a mentally defective boy, where the Board School Committee wrote to the parents requesting them to withdraw the boy from school entirely.

More about Drill

Military style drill was given in Board Schools after a conference with the War Office, when ex Army sergeants, from Brock Barracks in the case of Reading, were recommended as instructors.

Katesgrove Primary School, 1986
(Author).

The Reading School Board sanctioned the training of boys in military type drill when in 1876, a report from Coley School commented 'the boys went through the drill in capital style'. By 1899 the purely military–based concept was giving way to a more flexible, less rigid kind of physical exercise, which also included swimming instruction.

In the last years of the century, schools began to organise Football League fixtures with inter–school matches, a practice which in Reading has gone from strength to strength, testing and providing young footballers from the town schools for both county and international events.

The Teachers

Evidence for progress is to be found in the steady growth in the number of children taught, and in the gradual widening of their horizons through the subject matter of the curriculum. Above all, the dedication and quality of the local teaching force is reflected in H.M.I. and Head Teacher Reports. ' The children are well disciplined but the teaching and classwork are often far too loud.' is a comment from the summary of an Inspector's Report on Grovelands School for the school year ending 31 December, 1883.

A report on Newtown Board School by the H.M.I.s in January 1890 was full of praise:

'Boys School in excellent order... reading unusually good. Spelling satisfactory and Handwriting exceedingly neat throughout. Singing by note deserves good praise. Girls' School: tone and discipline very praiseworthy, infants are in very good order and have received highly satisfactory instructions in Object Lessons and elementary subjects.'

There were, however, occasional cases of grave indiscipline, of which the following quotation is one of the few lapses ever recorded:

'The order of the school broke up on Friday morning, 4 December, 1874 by Joseph Prior who defied my authority, was very abusive and tried to strike me with a shovel.' (This was presumably the implement used to replenish the heating stove, a tool I was personally responsible for in my early teaching days at a Dorset All Age School, where I was expected to teach and see to the stove in the winter months.). The report on Prior concludes 'He was not subdued until well birched.' (Silver Street Mixed Board School).

Opposite page top: *Katesgrove School Senior and Junior Football teams proudly display cups won for 1930–31.*
(C.L. Hibbert collection).

Opposite page lower: *Katesgrove Primary School viewed from east side, July 2002* *(Nigel Bray).*

K S B S
1930-31
WINNERS
SEN CUP
JUN CUP
SEN LGE
JUN LGE

Oxford Road Primary, formerly a Board School.
(R.S. Bray)

The rear of Grovelands School and showing the (former) Headmaster's house.
(R.S. Bray)

Other upsets came from parents who 'caused great unpleasantness' when their children were kept in after school, while in a dispute between the mother of a monitress and the certificated teacher in charge of the school, the Log Book records that the parent complained of the teacher that 'I held up my head as though I was someone superior, some lady of title.'

In another instance there was complete accord for one head teacher who reported 'I locked one boy in school by the parents' desire until 6 p.m. one evening, for playing truant in the morning.'

In terms of dedication, one Principal Teacher's attitude is typical of many others: 'I make but little progress in my own classes, owing to the backwardness of the children, and absences of the teachers. Standard Four is exceedingly backward, having to be left so often without a teacher. To get through the work, I am obliged to keep the dull children in. I hardly ever leave the school until one o'clock in the afternoon, and often I am teaching until 5.30 in the evening.'

Sometimes the situation was resolved by a direct appeal to the members of the Reading School Board as when the Principal Teacher at Coley Street School reported, 'the number of children has so increased that, in justice to myself and the school, I must ask for more efficient help than it is proposed to give me, viz. a monitor. Another one such as I already have would be of little use. What is really needed is a Transfer who has passed his 2nd Year examination, and without some assistance the school will not make the progress it ought to.'

Things were even more difficult at the Tilehurst Board School (later known as Grovelands School), when on the first opening on 6 December, 1880, Charles Tyler admitted '122 children without any assistance'. A pupil teacher in one Board School, with the help of a monitor, was supervising 67 boys in Standard Two, while 'Nellie Hookham, the monitress, was in charge of over 50 children including several babies'.

Financial Matters

Expenditure on teachers in Reading Board Schools for the year ending in September 1882 amounted to £1,229–7s–2d. At that time, the proposed salaries for teachers in the new Oxford Road School were, for a Principal Teacher in the Girls' Department £110 per annum for a 'fair' school, £125 for a 'good' school and £140 for an 'excellent' school.

Mr. Bibby, Principal Teacher at Coley Street School, wrote in the letter to the School Committee in January 1882, 'I cannot think that the Board have seen the injury it will do to me pecuniarily, and the injury also to the school', complaining about his financial loss, and the loss to the school by the proposed removal of his First Standard children to other premises.

The appointment of a new Headmaster (the term Principal

The First Board Schools

Teacher was used instead at this time) to Grovelands School was confirmed at £150 per annum, rising by increments of £7–10s to £172–10s, with a possible bonus at the end of each year of £120. This sum could be varied according to whether a Good, or Excellent Merit Grant was obtained, subject also to a deduction of £30 per annum for the occupation of the Teacher's Residence attached to the school.

A Katesgrove Infants' School Assistant Teacher was appointed at a salary of £50 per annum, one month's notice to be given on either side. Pupil Teachers appointed as Temporary Assistants received £25 per annum, while the Caretaker at the Oxford Road School, after an application for an increase in wages, was awarded £45 per annum. Bonus payments to some of the Principal Teachers in Board Schools under Article 101 of the Code, ranged in amounts varying from £6 to £40 for one year.

Well ahead of his time, one Reading Board Schools Committee member, Mr. Hodgson of the Social Democratic Federation, moved unsuccessfully at the 8 May, 1895 Committee Meeting, that the scales of salaries for teachers should be revised on the basis of equal remuneration for equal services, regardless of sex.

Training and Qualifications

Pupil teachers were allowed to go to College part time, and were occasionally given time off, part afternoons, for private study in connection with their examinations. The term apprenticeship for potential teachers was still being used as late as 1897. One H.M.I. Report in that year

Oxford Road School from Oxford Road side, July 2002.

(Nigel Bray)

noted that H. Lowe had not done well enough for admission to a shortened term of apprenticeship, while M.A. Gilbert was advised in the same report to pay attention to Composition and History. When a Pupil Teacher failed an examination, he or she was not automatically dismissed; a further year of grace might be allowed.

The University Extension College in Reading, together with the Reading School Board, was responsible for the instruction and examination of Pupil Teachers. The R.S.B. paid £2 per annum for each Pupil Teacher to the College, but for subjects like Drawing or Science, the students paid their own fees. Pupil Teachers appear to have served a five–year apprenticeship from the age of 13. For some, at the end of the road, was the possibility of a Queen's Scholarship for final qualification.

In 1896 the Board stated that it was having difficulty in obtaining sufficient numbers of Assistant Teachers. In spite of frequent advertisements in local and educational papers, some applicants were not suitably qualified, while others in the meantime had secured posts elsewhere.

Lessons

At St. Laurence's Infant School, animal lessons were on topics featuring Lions, Tigers, Whales, Camels and Bees. Object lesson themes centred on items such as a Clothes Brush, Milk, a Tea Pot, a piece of glass and a Toasting Fork.

Gradual but important changes took place in Reading Board Schools, due to pressures from the Education Department in London and the influence of the Cross Commission reports. * Efforts by individual teachers and Inspectors brought about the liberalising and widening of the curriculum, as in 1880 when the permitted list of classroom subjects was extended to include Chemistry.

In 1890 from the recommendations of the Cross Commission, drawing, science, physical education and manual work were allowed. At Grovelands School grant allocations per pupil were revised as follows: Principal Grant, 14s; Grant for Discipline, 1s; Singing, 1s; English and Elementary Science, 2s; Cookery, 4s.

At Oxford Road School in the Girls' Department, grants were allowed for Domestic Economy and Needlework, but slow learners who could not master the alphabet were not catered for, and some teachers did not want these pupils in their Infant classes.

A Mrs. Taplin refused to have one boy, because he was over seven years of age and would not make any progress with either figures or letters. 'I can do nothing with him here', she compained, an impasse which defied solution, as there was no means of helping children with special needs or disabilities. When inspecting the Silver Street School early in its history, one H.M.I. commented that 'the babies should have something more than the alphabet to interest them.'

The Cross Commission members reported that there were not enough reading books in some Board Schools and that too many reading lessons were turned into Spelling lessons. Towards the end of the Board School period, the Free Library in Reading was of some assistance to pupils starved of reading material.

Music consisted in the early days of singing unaccompanied, using a tuning fork, but in 1895 the Reading School Board decided to provide two pianos, one for the boys and one for the girls, in every school in place of harmoniums. The Board Chairman, Mr. J.H. Wilson, was against this innovation, saying that it was 'not a reasonable necessity', but the Rev. Ambrose Shepherd in moving the motion spoke of the hopeless poverty–cursed homes of some children, so that when he thought of 'the cruel emptiness of those children's lives, it seemed to him that pianos and music were matters of education and humanity'.

Children of about 13 or 14 were sometimes employed in Board Schools as monitors but the Head of Grovelands School in 1880 stated that 'monitors need as much looking after as the children they teach.' A grant was the incentive for the acceptance of Pupil Teachers, although their training involved school staff in a great deal of extra work. By 1889 the Reading School Board was concerned about the poor results of Pupil Teachers in examinations. It was also inclined, rightly or wrongly, to attribute some of the blame for this state of affairs to serving teachers.

The Board also introduced group instruction sessions for young female Pupil Teachers, six of whom it was recorded passed the Queen's Scolarship Examination for entry to a Teacher Training College. However, the attractiveness of teaching as a profession for men was observed to be decreasing steadily, and by 1902, the end of the Board School era, Pupil Teachers also were said to be fast becoming an 'extinct species'.

Grants

Over the years the single grant to Board Schools based on the constricting payment by results in the 3R's was supplemented by fee and aid grants. By 1891 a grant of 8s per child could be paid to those schools which reduced fees by that amount, or abolished school fees entirely.

Grant Aid continued to be used as a weapon by 'Their Lordships' of the Education Department in London, as in the case of St. Laurence's Infant School when in 1873 'Their Lordships' stated that under the Revised Code of 1863 twelve shillings per child was allowed, four shillings of which depended depended on regular, average attendance, the rest of the money on performance, or sufficient proficiency in the 3R's assessed via the visiting Inspector's annual examination.

Higher Tops

As the school syllabus broadened came provisions for evening classes, including 'Higher Tops' for girls and women at the Oxford Road School. Here in 1894, general basic subjects were available in the evening together with Needlework, History and Plain Cookery. Boys and men were able to take in addition to basic subjects, Geography, History and Book–keeping at the Central Boys' School. The Swansea Road Evening School (E.P. Collier Board School) issued a General Invitation, pointing out that 'these schools are intended chiefly for the benefit of scholars who are no longer subject to compulsory attendance at school, but who desire to prolong their education in order to fit themselves for industrial employment.'

'The Board invites these young persons (both boys and girls) who are leaving the Elementary Day Schools, to join these Evening Continuation Schools, and so to avail themselves of the advantages which a prolonged education in special subjects cannot fail to impart. The Board also invites the attendance of any other young persons, not having been scholars in the Elementary Schools, who may wish to join these Evening Schools.' Fees were 2d per week but the invitation added that 'one shilling in advance will secure the whole course in a subject, 2/6d for scholars in Advanced Needlework, Cookery or Advanced Dressmaking.'

Elementary Mechanics was taught in the Central Boys' School in 1895, while Chemistry was available there before 1900; in fact it had been possible since 1876 for Board Schools in many areas of the United Kingdom to introduce one or two 'extra' class subjects such as History or Geography, in addition to the required provision of instruction in the three R's.

All was not consistently sweetness and light, for as late as January 1890 an H.M.I. Report to the Reading School Board concerning Grovelands School stated that 'Grammar is pretty good in the 2nd and 3rd Standards, but so poor above this point that it is impossible to recommend a grant for English. To a somewhat less degree, the same remark applies to Geography, for which a grant is recommended with hesitation.'

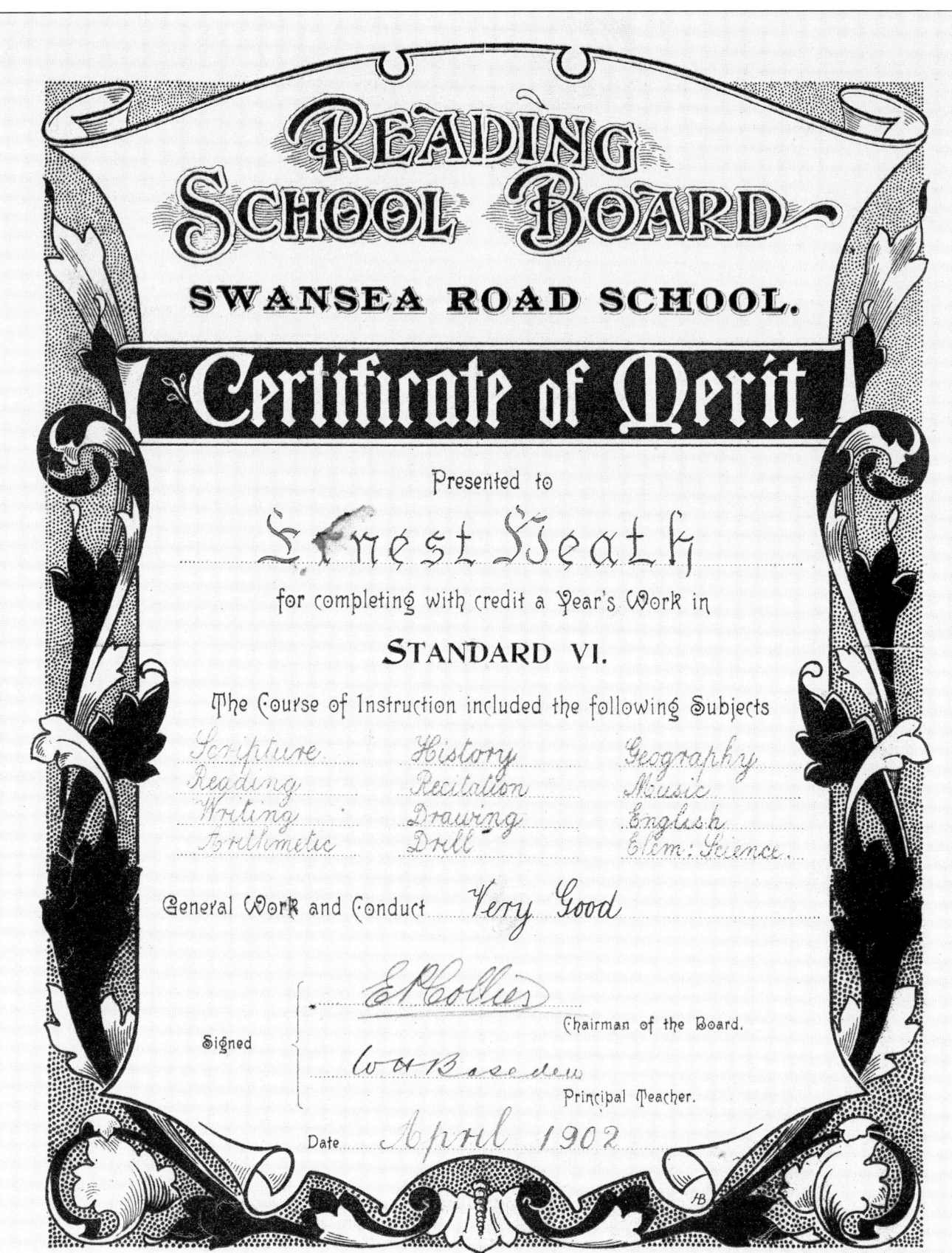

Chapter 4

THE PIONEERS

The history of education in Reading is linked to the names of the local elites who dominated town, school and council. The Palmers, Suttons, J.H. Wilson and E.P. Collier spring to mind immediately. A Mr. Samuel Collier brought his bride to their Minster Street house in 1836. He dealt in retailing pottery and glass, and was involved in the business of the Avenue Brickworks at Coley. His brother Edward (E.P. Collier) partnered him to the extent that Colliers became famous for specially distinctive hand–made bricks; outstanding examples of his decorated brickwork adorn many of the houses and other buildings still in existence in Reading. His name was given to the Swansea Road Board School opened on 16 January, 1899, an impressive piece of educational architecture with fine brickwork design, still towering over the sideways of Lower Caversham. Part of the main school bears the inscription Swansea Road Board School, while the separate entrances, originally one for Boys, another for Girls, are still visible. The school is known to this day as E.P. Collier School after 'E P C', a prominent member of Reading Education Committee who was appointed one of the Trustees of the Reading School Board in place of Joseph Henry Wilson, its first Chairman.

I am greatly indebted to the late Peter Shock, a former pupil of the school for information on the teething troubles of E.P. Collier School when at its opening, lack of sufficient blackboards meant that lessons had to be staggered. In its heyday it was an extremely popular and successful school, combining infant, junior and secondary departments with local children transferring easily from first to last in the same set of buildings, a state of affairs which in my personal opinion is sadly lacking today with the loss of school communities, our children transported in a bewildering manner of so–called choice from one end of the town to the other, with much disruption at peak travelling periods.

When it comes to other local worthies associated with education, here is just one tribute: 'The school will be called the Joseph Henry Wilson School after the first Chairman of the Reading School Board who remained in that office from 1871 to 1896, a period of twenty five years.'

Another great pioneer in Reading was Martin Hope Sutton (of Sutton's Seeds) who was invaluable as a teacher and superintendent in the 'Ragged School' movement as previously mentioned. Both he (brother of Alfred), and Mr. Palmer (of Huntley and Palmer's Biscuits) are remembered in the Sutton and Palmer Board Schools which bear their surnames, for they must rightly be praised for the enthusiasm and experience they brought into the first difficult years of elementary education in the town. They contributed both time and their own money in providing for the educational and welfare needs of the most destitute and neglected children.

The Military Men

The worthy efforts of the local businessmen turned philanthropists and educational innovators were aided by military men, retired officers including Major–General Jordan, Lieutenant–General McGregor and Lieutenant–Colonel Bazett, the two latter gentlemen being recorded in Board School Committee minutes as lecturing the boys 'concerning writing on the walls of the usual offices'.

On another occasion Colonel Bazett addressed the whole school (Coley Street) on the wrong doing of scholars, who when punished had run home and returned with abusive parents. Backward scholars were seen by General McGregor in September 1894, after which they were transferred to the Infants' Department of the Coley Street School from Standard One.

Engraved letter 'Swansea Road Board School' on the top storey of E.P. Collier School, 1986.

(Author)

Top:
E.P. Collier School from Swansea Road, July 2002.
(Nigel Bray)

Left;
Wilson School viewed from Wilson Road, July 2002.
(Nigel Bray)

Above: Wilson Junior Girls School, Standard II, c. 1928. (Mrs. V. Heaton collection)

Lower: 12–13 year olds at E.P. Collier School, 1936. (Mrs. G. Day collection)

Reading's Forgotten Children

Above:

Alfred Sutton primary school, formerly Wokingham Road Board School, July 2002. *(Nigel Bray)*

Left:

Alfred Sutton primary school from the playground, July 2002.
(Nigel Bray)

George Palmer School, from car park, July 2002. (Nigel Bray).

In Conclusion

The 1870 Education Act was a compromise designed to assist and placate a number of rival vested intersts. Intended to fill gaps in 'voluntary' educational provision, it resulted gradually in replacing the former systems almost entirely; often, quite accidentally, the Board Schools stimulated local initiatives and innovations, rather than from 'state' directives on high, a trend which hopefully will continue as the way forward in education.

The Rev. Henry Moseley (H.M.I.) wrote in 1846 words which sadly reflected educational reality then and for many years after, 'We break off a fragment from the education we suppose necessary for <u>our own</u> children, its mechanical and technical part – and give it to the poor man's child in charity.'

Yet by 1891 free education was given a place in the Government's programme, while grants for education and science were by then counted in millions of pounds. By 1900 the number of Reading pupils on Board School Registers was nearly three thousand above the number of children on the registers of all other schools in Reading.

It was time for a change, which followed fairly quickly arising out of a test case which when passed through the law courts decreed that the efforts of local School Boards to extend their lessons to cover some form of secondary education were illegal. This, the Cockerton judgment of 1899 prompted what in our language is termed a rethink, resulting in a complete overhaul and replacement of the old order through the Balfour Education Act of 1902.

School Boards set up from 1870 (1871 in Reading) were to be abolished, their duties and responsibilities becoming the educational concern of County and Borough Councils. The Act of 1870 had left the country with a confused and often inefficient state of affairs in which all kinds of academies were financed, propped up and suffered to flourish or decline with fees, donations and small state grants dating back in some cases to the settlements of 1833. Under the provisions of the Balfour Act the voluntary schools were to be state aided, which meant more control and more effective supervision of schools and teachers, leading eventually to a levelling up of finances and teaching salaries.

After thirty years of struggling, the ordinary schools were now secure. With the passing of the Balfour Act the Board Schools ceased to exist, the stigma of Board School education disappeared, the label elementary education lingered on, but the dedication of the teachers and the administrators, ensured that the schools in Reading inherited and developed a fine record of endeavour, one to be proud of in the twentieth century and beyond.

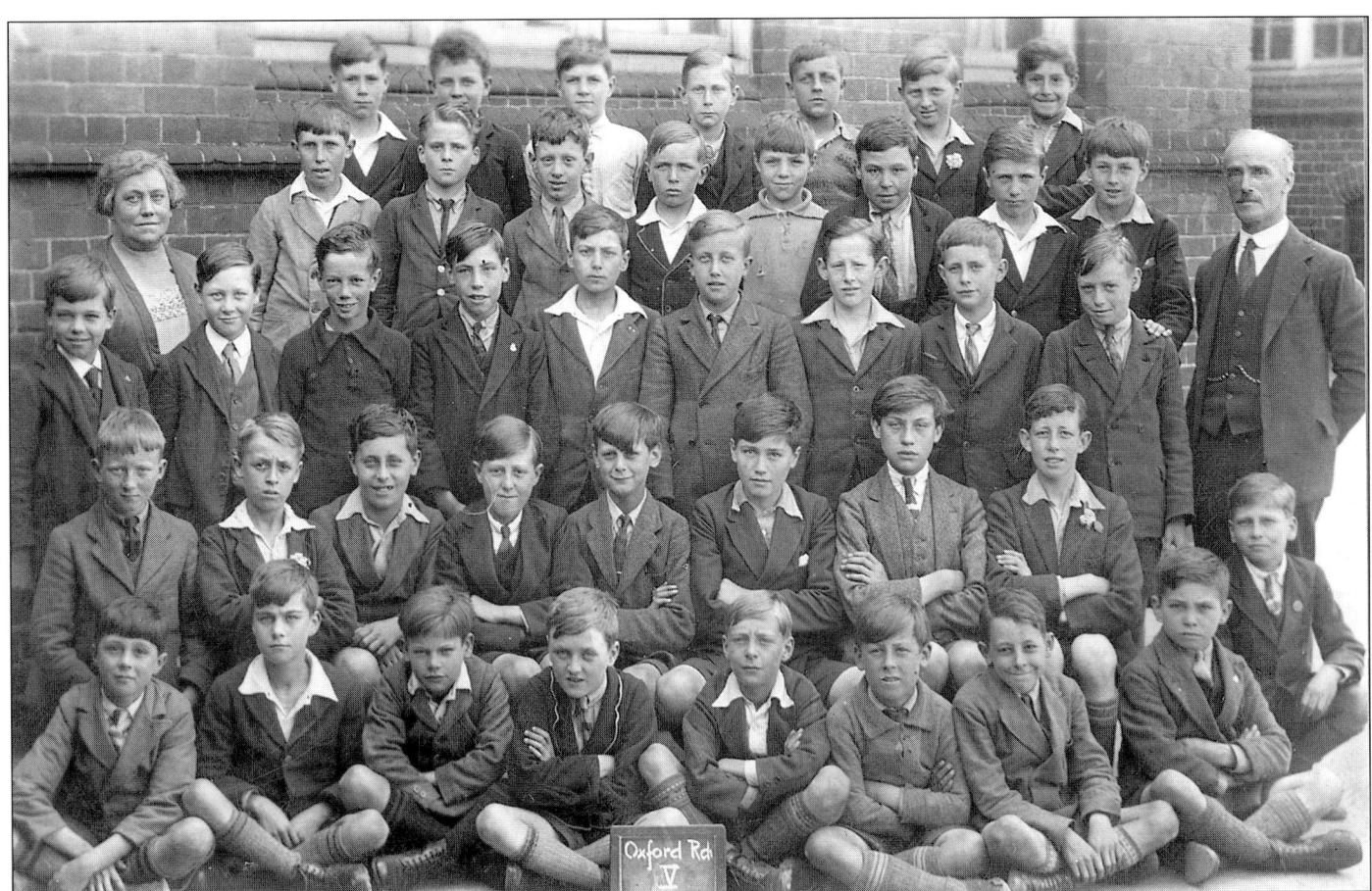

Boys at Oxford Road Junior School, Year Five, 1929. *(Victor Day collection)*

APPENDIX 1

Reading Board Schools in 1902, as listed in Kelly's Directory for Reading, 1903.

Battle School (mixed), opened 1893 at junction of Kensington Road and Prince of Wales Avenue, West Reading.

Central (Boys) School, opened in 1891 in Orchard Street, Katesgrove.

Coley Street School, opened 1874 to replace temporary classroooms opened in 1871.

Grovelands School, opened in 1880 (then in Tilehurst Parish) at junction of Grovelands Road and Oxford Road, West Reading. Transferred to Reading School Board when Borough boundary was enlarged in 1887.

Katesgrove School (girls and infants), opened in 1873 in Katesgrove Lane and reconstructed in 1891.

Newtown School, opened in 1874 in School Terrace, between Cholmeley Road and Cumberland Road, East Reading.

Oxford Road School, opened in 1883 at junction of George Street and Oxford Road, West Reading.

Redlands, opened in 1892 in Lydford Road, East Reading.

Silver Street School, opened in 1872, at junction of Silver Street and Eagle Court.

Southampton Street School, between Lily Place and Mount Place.

Swansea Road (later known as E.P. Collier School), opened in 1899 between Swansea Road and York Road.

Wokingham Road (later known as Alfred Sutton School), along Wokingham Road between its junctions with Crescent Road and Green Road, East Reading.

APPENDIX 2

Average Attendance at Reading Board Schools in the year up to 31 October, 1902, as shown in Kelly's Directory for Reading, 1903.

Name of School	Accommodation for number of children	Average attendance
Southampton Street	801	499
Coley Street	608	523
Katesgrove	629	562
Silver Street	236	140
Oxford Road	1000	915
Newtown	1455	1313
Grovelands	570	533
Redlands	1166	1018
Battle	1132	1019
Central (Boys)	466	411
Swansea Road	990	801
Wokingham Road	560	317
Total	**9613**	**8051**

REFERENCES

Reading Board Schools Committee Minute Books, 1871–1902.

Peter Shock, The Collier Story (Reading Central Reference Library).

D.F. Chandler, A History of Grovelands School.

T. Babbage, Tylehurst Described.

Professor W. Harman, A History of Education in Reading (Reading Central Reference Library).

J.W. Dicking, Schools and Scholars, Coventry & North Warwickshire History Pamphlet No. 3.

Gillian Sutherland, Elementary Education in the 19th Century, Historical Association.

The Educational Crisis in Salisbury, 1888–90, Wiltshire Archaeological & Natural History Magazine, Volume 78 (1984), pp 87–91.

Industrialisation and Culture, Open University.

Hansard Series (iii) Volume 199, columns 465–66.

Brian Simon, Studies in the History of Education (1780–1870), Chapter 7.

Sir H.M. Maxwell, Bart., Sixty Years a Queen, Eyre & Spottiswood, 1897.

G.M. Young, Victorian England.

Rear cover photo: E. P. Collier School. Note the lettering displaying its original name of Swansea Road Board School, July 2002. Several nearby houses were sporting 'Save our Local Schools' posters. The school has since been reprieved.
(Nigel Bray).